Before you start ...

1 Gather together everything you need for the activity using the equipment list at the top of each page. Collect lots of different materials, from seashells to bottle tops, that you can use for making things.

2 Cover your work table with newspaper and wear an apron to protect your clothes.

3 Read all the instructions carefully. Always wait for glue and paint to dry.

4 Be very careful with scissors and knives. Only use them if an adult is there to help you.

5 When you have finished an activity, wash your hands and put everything away.

DK

A DORLING KINDERSLEY BOOK

Written and edited by Dawn Sirett and Lara Tankel
Art Editors Mandy Earey and Mary Sandberg
Additional design Veneta Altham
Deputy Managing Art Editor C. David Gillingwater
Production Fiona Baxter and Jo Blackmore
Dib, Dab, and Dob made by Wilfrid Wood
Photography by Alex Wilson and Norman Hollands
Illustrations by Peter Kavanagh
Spoon puppets, fish, and monster made by Jane Bull

First published in Great Britain in 1997
by Dorling Kindersley Limited,
9 Henrietta Street, London WC2E 8PS

Copyright © 1997 Dorling Kindersley Limited, London

Visit us on the World Wide Web at http://www.dk.com

A CIP catalogue record for this book is
available from the British Library.

ISBN 0-7513-5574-7

Colour reproduction by Colourscan, Singapore
Printed and bound in Hong Kong by Imago

PLAY AND LEARN
Making things

With Dib, Dab, and Dob

DORLING KINDERSLEY
London • New York • Stuttgart • Moscow

paint  paintbrush wooden spoon card scissors

Turn spoons into puppets

Paint a design on a wooden spoon.

Cut legs or ears from card and glue them on.

Glue on pipe cleaners or wool for hair, horns, or antennae.

 scissors coloured cord dried pasta tubes

Turn pasta into jewellery

Cut a length of cord a little longer than you want your necklace to be.

I've tied a knot in one end of the cord to stop the pasta falling off.

Thread pasta tubes on to the cord.

Finally, tie the ends together to make a necklace.

I've used beads and made a bracelet, too.

Make a flying fish

Fold a square of tissue paper in half. Draw a fish on the paper with a big mouth and tail.

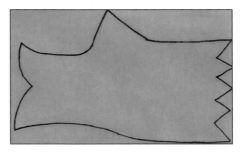

Cut out the fish. Glue the long sides together, leaving the tail and mouth open.

clear tape   hole punch   thin wool

Decorate each side of the fish.

It's nearly finished now, Dib.

Stick tape on the corners of the mouth on both sides of the fish. Punch holes through the taped corners.

Up, up, and away!

Thread the ends of a long length of wool through the holes you have made. Tie a knot in each one.

The tape will stop the holes from tearing.

Try making other designs. A rocket works well.

To make your fish fly,
hold the wool and run
around quickly.

rice

two
plastic cups

masking
tape

PVA
glue

buttons

Make noisy shakers

Pour some rice
into a plastic cup.

That should
be enough.

Turn another cup
upside down and
tape it to the first cup.

ribbon pipe cleaners wool sweet wrappers felt

Glue on buttons, ribbon,
pipe cleaners, wool, felt,
or sweet wrappers
for decoration.

Now shake along to your favourite songs.

Wind wool to make a pompom

Ask an adult to cut out two card rings. The rings need to be the same size.

Wind the wool through the hole and round the ring.

Hold the rings together and wind lengths of wool round them. When you reach the end of a length, knot it to a new one and keep winding.

felt

pipe cleaners

Stop when you can't wind on any more wool. Then ask an adult to cut through the wool, as shown.

Cut through the wool round the edge of the rings.

Then wrap a long length of wool between the two card rings and tie a tight knot. Pull off the rings.

Pompom party

Stick on toy eyes, felt, and
pipe cleaners to transform
your pompom into a pet.

Try threading pompoms
together to make
a hairy caterpillar.

What sort of
pet are you going
to make?

empty boxes paint paintbrush PVA glue torn paper

Make a rubbish monster

Find some empty boxes that you can use to make a monster. Paint them and leave them to dry.

Then glue the boxes together to make a monster shape.

buttons felt

Finally, glue on paper, buttons, or felt to create the monster's skin.

Oh no! I think it's hungry.